WONDERFUL NATURAL WONDERS

THE MISSISSIPPI RIVER

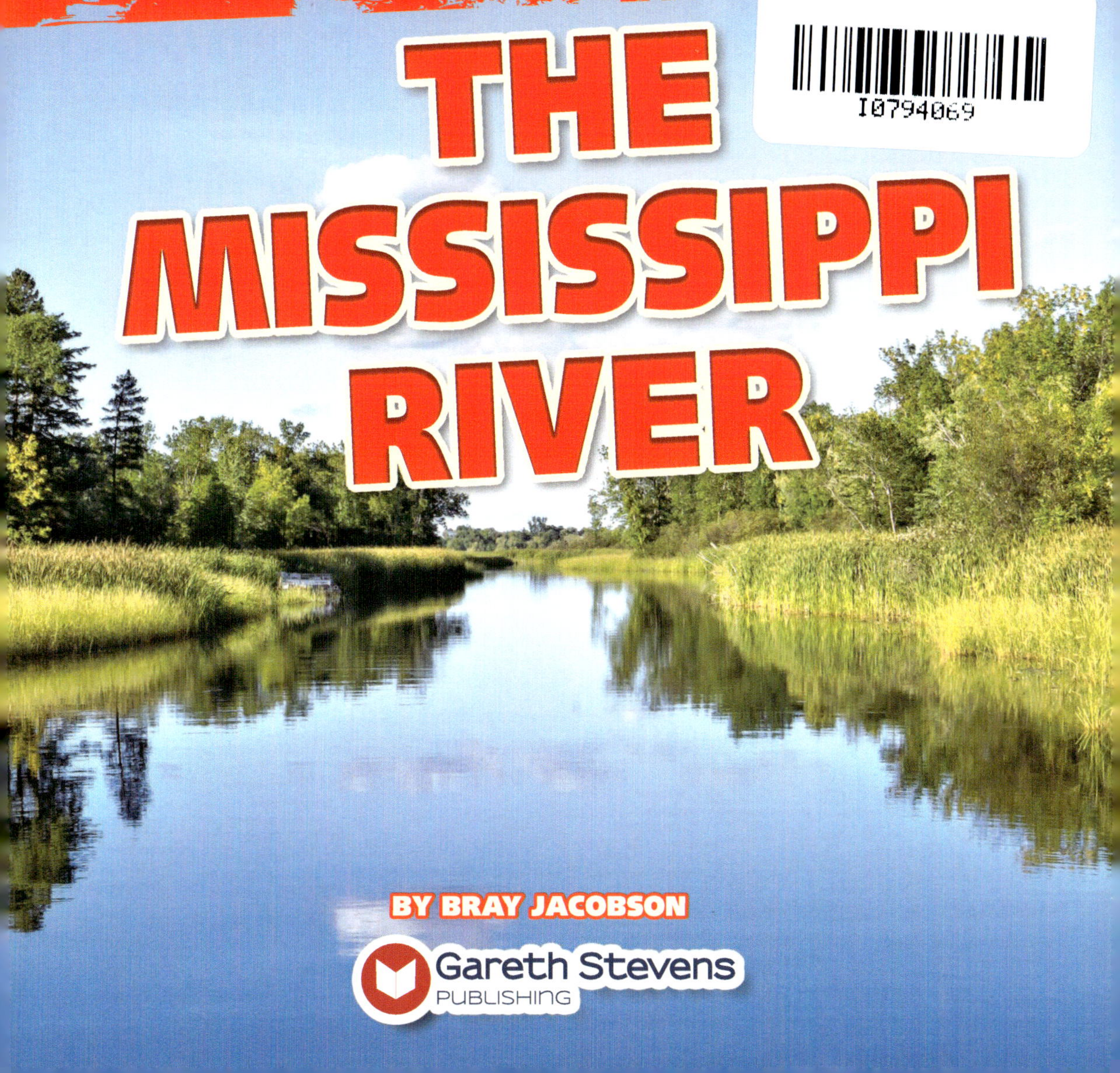

BY BRAY JACOBSON

Gareth Stevens PUBLISHING

Please visit our website, www.garethstevens.com. For a free color catalog of all our high-quality books, call toll free 1-800-542-2595 or fax 1-877-542-2596.

Library of Congress Cataloging-in-Publication Data

Names: Jacobson, Bray, author.
Title: The Mississippi River / Bray Jacobson.
Description: New York : Gareth Stevens Publishing, 2023. | Series: Wonderful natural wonders | Includes index.
Identifiers: LCCN 2021036584 (print) | LCCN 2021036585 (ebook) | ISBN 9781538276822 (set) | ISBN 9781538276839 (library binding) | ISBN 9781538276815 (paperback) | ISBN 9781538276846 (ebook)
Subjects: LCSH: Mississippi River–Juvenile literature.
Classification: LCC F351 .J34 2023 (print) | LCC F351 (ebook) | DDC 977–dc23
LC record available at https://lccn.loc.gov/2021036584
LC ebook record available at https://lccn.loc.gov/2021036585

Published in 2023 by
Gareth Stevens Publishing
29 E. 21st Street
New York, NY 10010

Designer: Tanya Dellaccio
Editor: Kristen Nelson

Photo credits: Cover Edgar Lee Espe/Shutterstock.com; background texture (pp 3-24) BEMPhoto_31/ Shutterstock.com; p. 5 Joseph Sohm/Shutterstock.com; pp. 7, 13 Bardocz Peter/Shutterstock.com; p. 9 Nancy Bauer/Shutterstock.com; p. 11 LDEV31/Shutterstock.com; p. 15 marekuliasz/Shutterstock.com; p. 17 Bonita R. Cheshier/Shutterstock.com; p. 19 Katie Flenker/Shutterstock.com; p. 21 Suzanne Tucker/ Shutterstock.com.

Printed in the United States of America

CPSIA compliance information: Batch #CSGS23: For further information contact Gareth Stevens, New York, New York at 1-800-542-2595.

CONTENTS

Boldface words appear in the glossary.

The Mighty Mississippi

The Mississippi is one of the longest rivers in the United States. Its length is only part of why it's a natural wonder. The Mississippi River is also a big part of a huge **system** of other bodies of water.

Along the River

The Mississippi River starts as a small stream in Minnesota, flowing out from Lake Itasca. It passes through 10 states, including Iowa, Illinois, and Louisiana. The river empties into the Gulf of Mexico. It carries more water than any other U.S. river!

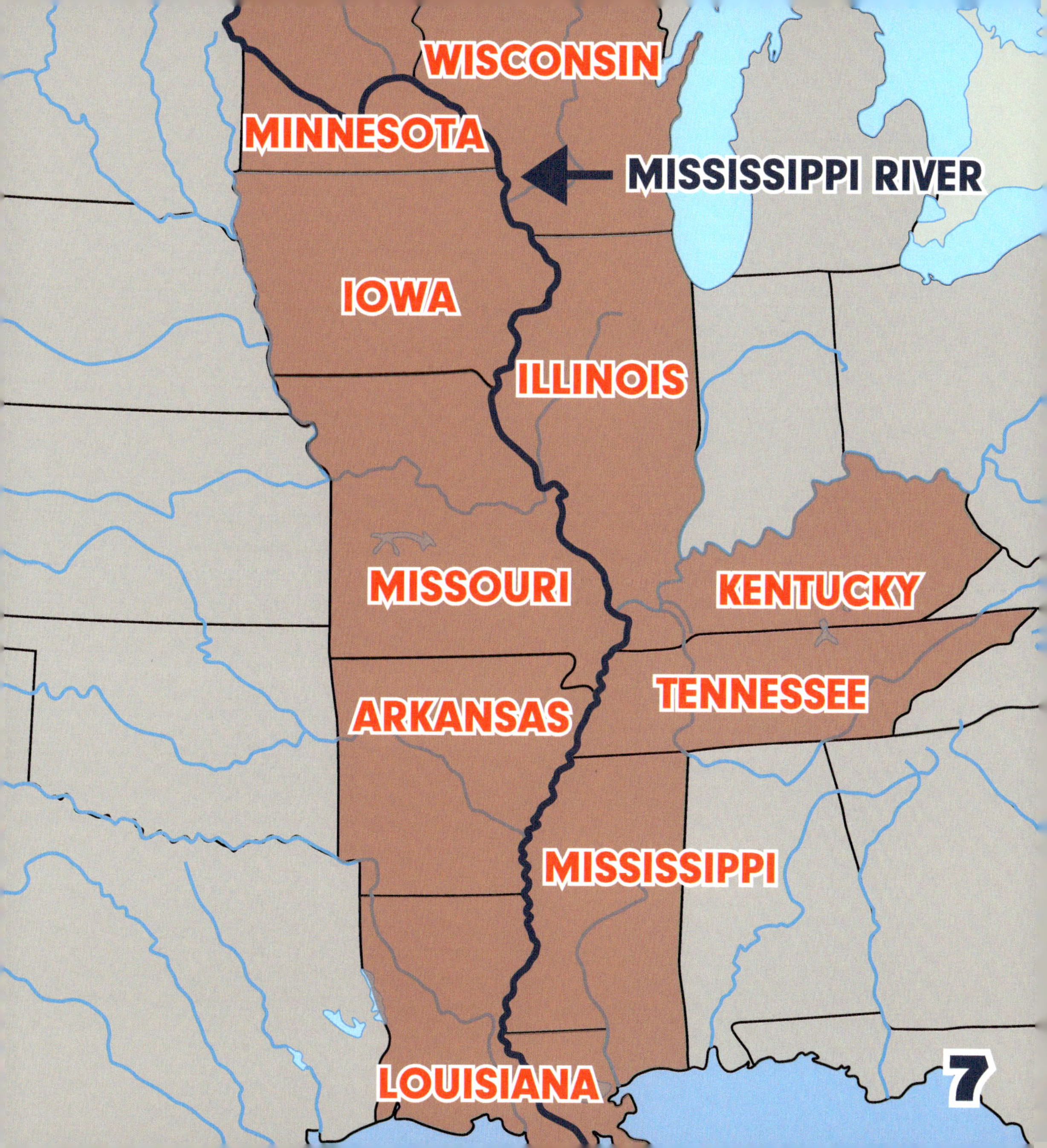
WISCONSIN
MINNESOTA
MISSISSIPPI RIVER
IOWA
ILLINOIS
MISSOURI
KENTUCKY
TENNESSEE
ARKANSAS
MISSISSIPPI
LOUISIANA

The Mississippi River is about 2,350 miles (3,782 km) long. That makes it the second-longest river in North America. The Missouri River is longer by about 100 miles (160 km). The Mississippi River is also the fourth-longest river in the world.

The Mississippi River starts out as only about 20 to 30 feet (6 to 9 m) wide near Lake Itasca. But, it's 11 miles (18 km) across at its widest! In many places, bridges have been built so cars and even trains can cross it.

The Whole System

The Mississippi River system has 250 **tributaries**! The Missouri, Arkansas, Red, Illinois, and Ohio Rivers are all tributaries of the Mississippi. They're long rivers themselves! They have tributaries that are part of the Mississippi River system too.

MISSISSIPPI RIVER
MISSOURI RIVER
ILLINOIS RIVER
OHIO RIVER
ARKANSAS RIVER
RED RIVER

Useful Waters

Altogether, the Mississippi River system has about 12,000 miles (19,000 km) of waterways people can use. The system has far-reaching effects. Its **watershed** includes 32 states and even parts of Canada! Millions of people rely on the river system for their drinking water.

MISSISSIPPI RIVER MEETING THE MISSOURI RIVER

The waters of the Mississippi River system are surrounded by **fertile** farmland. The Mississippi River has also long been part of the shipping industry. Goods are moved on boats that travel down the Mississippi and its tributaries.

Wildlife

The natural wonder that is the Mississippi River is important to plants and animals too. More than 100 kinds of fish live in the Mississippi River, including bass, bluegill, and northern pike. The river is also known for the birds that **migrate** near it.

PELICAN

River Parks

There are many parks along the length of the Mississippi. They **protect** the river and area around it as well as share its beauty. The Mississippi National River and **Recreation** Area in Minnesota is 72 miles (116 km) long!

GLOSSARY

fertile: able to support the growth of many crops

migrate: to move from one area to another at different times of the year

protect: to keep safe

recreation: having to do with activities people do for fun

system: a group of parts that work together

tributary: a river or stream that flows into another, often larger, river, stream, or lake.

watershed: the land that includes a certain river or lake and all the rivers, streams, or other bodies of water that flow into it

FOR MORE INFORMATION

BOOKS

Adil, Janeen R. *Mississippi River.* New York, NY: AV2, 2021.

Brereton, Catherine. *Rivers of the World.* Oxford, UK: Raintree, 2018.

WEBSITES

Mississippi River Facts
www.nps.gov/miss/riverfacts.htm
Check out facts about the Mississippi River from the National Park Service.

Mississippi River Facts for Kids
www.coolkidfacts.com/mississippi-river/
Read more fun facts about the mighty Mississippi!

INDEX